The Key Facts™
on North Korea

Essential Information on North Korea
By Patrick W. Nee

The Internationalist®
www.internationalist.com
This is the best available information on North Korea

The Internationalist®

International Business, Investment, and Travel

Published by:

The Internationalist Publishing Company

96 Walter Street/ Suite 200

Boston, MA 02131, USA

Tel: 617-354-7722

www.internationalist.com

PN@internationalist.com

Table Of Contents

Chapter 1: Introduction and Background:

An independent kingdom for much of its long history, Korea was occupied by Japan beginning in 1905 following the Russo-Japanese War. Five years later, Japan formally annexed the entire peninsula. Following World War II, Korea was split with the northern half coming under Soviet-sponsored Communist control. After failing in the Korean War (1950-53) to conquer the US-backed Republic of Korea (ROK) in the southern portion by force, North Korea (DPRK), under its founder President KIM Il Sung, adopted a policy of ostensible diplomatic and economic "self-reliance" as a check against outside influence. The DPRK demonized the US as the ultimate threat to its social system through state-funded propaganda, and molded political, economic, and military policies around the core ideological objective of eventual unification of Korea under Pyongyang's control. KIM Il Sung's son, KIM Jong Il, was officially designated as his father's successor in 1980, assuming a growing political and managerial role until the elder KIM's death in 1994. KIM Jong Un was publicly unveiled as his father's successor in September 2010. Following KIM Jong Il's death in December 2011, the regime began to take actions to transfer power to KIM Jong Un and Jong Un has begun to assume his father's former titles and duties. After decades of economic mismanagement and resource misallocation, the DPRK since the mid-1990s has relied heavily on international aid to feed its population. North Korea's history of regional military provocations, proliferation of military-related items, long-range missile development, WMD programs including tests of nuclear devices in 2006 and 2009, and massive conventional armed forces are of major concern to the international community. The regime has marked 2012, the centenary of KIM Il Sung's birth, a banner year; to that end, the country has heightened its focus on developing its economy and improving its people's livelihoods.

Chapter 2: Geography

Location:

Eastern Asia, northern half of the Korean Peninsula bordering the Korea Bay and the Sea of Japan, between China and South Korea

Geographic coordinates:

40 00 N, 127 00 E

Map references:

Asia

Area:

total: 120,538 sq km

country comparison to the world: 99

land: 120,408 sq km

water: 130 sq km

Area - comparative:

slightly smaller than Mississippi

Land boundaries:

total: 1,671.5 km

border countries: China 1,416 km, South Korea 238 km, Russia 17.5 km

Coastline:

2,495 km

Maritime claims:

territorial sea: 12 nm

exclusive economic zone: 200 nm

note: military boundary line 50 nm in the Sea of Japan and the exclusive economic zone limit in the Yellow Sea where all foreign vessels and aircraft without permission are banned

Climate:

temperate with rainfall concentrated in summer

Terrain:

mostly hills and mountains separated by deep, narrow valleys; coastal plains wide in west, discontinuous in east

Elevation extremes:

lowest point: Sea of Japan 0 m

highest point: Paektu-san 2,744 m

Natural resources:

coal, lead, tungsten, zinc, graphite, magnesite, iron ore, copper, gold, pyrites, salt, fluorspar, hydropower

Land use:

arable land: 22.4%

permanent crops: 1.66%

other: 75.94% (2005)

Irrigated land:

14,600 sq km (2003)

Total renewable water resources:

77.1 cu km (1999)

Freshwater withdrawal (domestic/industrial/agricultural):

total: 9.02 cu km/yr (20%/25%/55%)

per capita: 401 cu m/yr (2000)

Natural hazards:

late spring droughts often followed by severe flooding; occasional typhoons during the early fall

volcanism: Changbaishan (elev. 2,744 m) (also known as Baitoushan, Baegdu or P'aektu-san), on the Chinese border, is considered historically active

Environment - current issues:

water pollution; inadequate supplies of potable water; waterborne disease; deforestation; soil erosion and degradation

Environment - international agreements:

party to: Antarctic Treaty, Biodiversity, Climate Change, Climate Change-Kyoto Protocol, Desertification, Environmental Modification, Hazardous Wastes, Ozone Layer Protection, Ship Pollution

signed, but not ratified: Law of the Sea

Geography - note:

strategic location bordering China, South Korea, and Russia; mountainous interior is isolated and sparsely populated

Chapter 3: People and Society

Nationality:

noun: Korean(s)

adjective: Korean

Ethnic groups:

racially homogeneous; there is a small Chinese community and a few ethnic Japanese

Languages:

Korean

Religions:

traditionally Buddhist and Confucianist, some Christian and syncretic Chondogyo (Religion of the Heavenly Way)

note: autonomous religious activities now almost nonexistent; government-sponsored religious groups exist to provide illusion of religious freedom

Population:

24,589,122 (July 2012 est.)

country comparison to the world: 49

Age structure:

0-14 years: 22% (male 2,742,874/female 2,672,199)

15-24 years: 16.5% (male 2,060,206/female 1,998,436)

25-54 years: 44% (male 5,402,999/female 5,416,701)

55-64 years: 8.2% (male 942,529/female 1,064,570)

65 years and over: 9.3% (male 768,703/female 1,519,905) (2012 est.)

Median age:

total: 33 years

male: 31.4 years

female: 34.7 years (2012 est.)

Population growth rate:

0.535% (2012 est.)

country comparison to the world: 149

Birth rate:

14.51 births/1,000 population (2012 est.)

country comparison to the world: 137

Death rate:

9.12 deaths/1,000 population (July 2012 est.)

country comparison to the world: 65

Net migration rate:

-0.04 migrant(s)/1,000 population (2012 est.)

country comparison to the world: 116

Urbanization:

urban population: 60% of total population (2010)

rate of urbanization: 0.6% annual rate of change (2010-15 est.)

Sex ratio:

at birth: 1.05 male(s)/female

under 15 years: 1.03 male(s)/female

15-64 years: 0.99 male(s)/female

65 years and over: 0.51 male(s)/female

total population: 0.94 male(s)/female (2011 est.)

Maternal mortality rate:

81 deaths/100,000 live births (2010)

country comparison to the world: 82

Infant mortality rate:

total: 26.21 deaths/1,000 live births

country comparison to the world: 76

male: 29.05 deaths/1,000 live births

female: 23.24 deaths/1,000 live births (2012 est.)

Life expectancy at birth:

total population: 69.2 years

country comparison to the world: 152

male: 65.34 years

female: 73.24 years (2012 est.)

Total fertility rate:

2.01 children born/woman (2012 est.)

country comparison to the world: 130

Health expenditures:

2% of GDP (2009)

country comparison to the world: 189

Physicians density:

3.29 physicians/1,000 population (2003)

Hospital bed density:

13.2 beds/1,000 population (2002)

Sanitation facility access:

improved:

urban: 58% of population

rural: 60% of population

total: 59% of population

unimproved:

urban: 42% of population

rural: 40% of population

total: 41% of population

Children under the age of 5 years underweight:

20.6% (2004)

country comparison to the world: 33

Literacy:

definition: age 15 and over can read and write

total population: 99%

male: 99%

<u>female</u>: 99% (1991 est.)

Chapter 4: Government

Country name:

> conventional long form: Democratic People's Republic of Korea

> conventional short form: North Korea

> local long form: Choson-minjujuui-inmin-konghwaguk

> local short form: Choson

> abbreviation: DPRK

Government type:

> Communist state one-man dictatorship

Capital:

> name: Pyongyang

> geographic coordinates: 39 01 N, 125 45 E

> time difference: UTC+9 (14 hours ahead of Washington, DC during Standard Time)

Administrative divisions:

> 9 provinces (do, singular and plural) and 2 municipalities (si, singular and plural)

> provinces: Chagang-do (Chagang), Hamgyong-bukto (North Hamgyong), Hamgyong-namdo (South Hamgyong), Hwanghae-bukto (North Hwanghae), Hwanghae-namdo (South Hwanghae), Kangwon-do (Kangwon), P'yongan-bukto (North P'yongan), P'yongan-namdo (South P'yongan), Yanggang-do (Yanggang)

> municipalities: Nason-si, P'yongyang-si (Pyongyang)

Independence:

15 August 1945 (from Japan)

National holiday:

Founding of the Democratic People's Republic of Korea (DPRK), 9 September (1948)

Constitution:

adopted 1948; revised several times

Legal system:

civil law system based on the Prussian model; system influenced by Japanese traditions and Communist legal theory

International law organization participation:

has not submitted an ICJ jurisdiction declaration; non-party state to the ICCt

Suffrage:

17 years of age; universal

Executive branch:

chief of state: KIM Jong Un (since 17 December 2011)

note - the rubberstamp Supreme People's Assembly (SPA) reelected KIM Yong Nam in 2009 president of its Presidium also with responsibility of representing state and receiving diplomatic credentials

head of government: Premier CHOE Yong Rim (since 7 June 2010); Vice Premiers: HAN Kwang Bok (since 7 June 2010), JO Pyong Ju (since 7 June 2010), JON Ha Chol (since 7 June 2010), KANG Nung Su (since 7 June 2010), KANG Sok Ju (since 23 September 2010), KIM In Sik (since 13 April 2012), KIM Rak Hui (since 7 June 2010), KIM Yong Jin (since 6 January 2012), PAK Su Gil (since 18 September 2009), RI Chol Man (since 13 April

2012), RI Mu Yong (since 31 May 2011), RI Sung Ho (since 13 April 2012), RO Tu Chol (since 3 September 2003)

cabinet: Naegak (cabinet) members, except for Minister of People's Armed Forces, are appointed by SPA

elections: last election held in April 2012; date of next election NA

election results: KIM Jong Un elected

Legislative branch:

unicameral Supreme People's Assembly or Ch'oego Inmin Hoeui (687 seats; members elected by popular vote to serve five-year terms)

elections: last held on 8 March 2009 (next to be held in March 2014)

election results: percent of vote by party - NA; seats by party - NA; ruling party approves a list of candidates who are elected without opposition; a token number of seats are reserved for minor parties

Judicial branch:

Central Court (judges are elected by the Supreme People's Assembly)

Political parties and leaders:

major party - Korean Workers' Party or KWP [KIM Jong Un]; minor parties - Chondoist Chongu Party [RYU Mi Yong] (under KWP control), Social Democratic Party [KIM Yong Dae] (under KWP control)

Key Leaders:

Eternal Gen. Sec., Korean Workers' Party (KWP)	KIM Jong Il

First Sec., KWP	KIM Jong Un
Eternal Chmn., National Defense Commission (NDC)	KIM Jong Il
First Chmn., NDC	KIM Jong Un
Supreme Cdr., Korean People's Army (KPA)	KIM Jong Un
First Vice Chmn., NDC	
Vice Chmn., NDC	JANG Song Thaek
Vice Chmn., NDC	KIM Yong Chun
Vice Chmn., NDC	O Kuk Ryol
Vice Chmn., NDC	RI Yong Mu
Member, NDC	CHOE Ryong Hae
Member, NDC	JU Kyu Chang
Member, NDC	KIM Jong Gak
Member, NDC	KIM Won Hong
Member, NDC	PAEK Se Bong
Member, NDC	PAK To Chun
Member, NDC	RI Myong Su

Councilor, NDC	PAK Myong Chol
Min. of People's Armed Forces (directly subordinate to the NDC)	KIM Jong Gak
Pres., Supreme People's Assembly (SPA) Presidium	KIM Yong Nam
Vice Pres., SPA Presidium	KIM Yong Dae
Vice Pres., SPA Presidium	YANG Hyong Sop
Honorary Vice Pres., SPA Presidium	KIM Yong Ju
Sec. Gen., SPA Presidium	PYON Yong Rip
Sec. Gen., SPA Presidium	THAE Hyong Chol
Member, SPA Presidium	HONG Sok Hyong
Member, SPA Presidium	KANG Chang Uk
Member, SPA Presidium	KANG Yong Sop
Member, SPA	KIM Pyong

Presidium	Phal
Member, SPA Presidium	KIM Yang Gon
Member, SPA Presidium	RI Yong Chol
Member, SPA Presidium	RO Song Sil
Member, SPA Presidium	RYU Mi Yong
Member, SPA Presidium	SIM Sang Jin
Member, SPA Presidium	THAE Hyong Chol
Chmn., SPA	CHOE Thae Bok
Vice Chmn., SPA	HONG Son Ok
Vice Chmn., SPA	KIM Wan Su
Premier, Cabinet	CHOE Yong Rim
Vice Premier, Cabinet	HAN Kwang Bok
Vice Premier, Cabinet	JO Pyong Ju
Vice Premier, Cabinet	JON Ha Chol
Vice Premier, Cabinet	KANG Nung

	Su
Vice Premier, Cabinet	KANG Sok Ju
Vice Premier, Cabinet	KIM In Sik
Vice Premier, Cabinet	KIM Rak Hui
Vice Premier, Cabinet	KIM Yong Jin
Vice Premier, Cabinet	PAK Su Gil
Vice Premier, Cabinet	RI Chol Man
Vice Premier, Cabinet	RI Mu Yong
Vice Premier, Cabinet	RI Sung Ho
Vice Premier, Cabinet	RO Tu Chol
Chief, Cabinet Secretariat	KIM Yong Ho
Min. of Agriculture	KIM Chang Sik
Min. of Capital City Construction	KIM Ung Gwan
Min. of Chemical Industry	RI Mu Yong
Min. of Coal Industry	KIM Hyong Sik
Min. of Commerce	KIM Pong Chol

Min. of Construction & Building-Materials Industries	TONG Jong Ho
Min. of Culture	AN Tong Chun
Min. of Electric Power Industry	HO Thaek
Min. of Electronics Industry	HAN Kwang Bok
Min. of Finance	PAK Su Gil
Min. of Fisheries	PAK Thae Won
Min. of Foodstuffs & Daily Necessities Industry	JO Yong Chol
Min. of Foreign Affairs	PAK Ui Chun
Min. of Foreign Trade	RI Ryong Nam
Min. of Forestry	KIM Kwang Yong
Min. of Labor	JONG Yong Su
Min. of Land & Environment Preservation	KIM Chang Ryong
Min. of Land & Marine Transport	RA Tong Hui
Min. of Light Industry	AN Jong Su

Min. of Machine-Building Industry	JO Pyong Ju
Min. of Metal Industry	KIM Thae Bong
Min. of Mining Industry	KANG Min Chol
Min. of Oil Industry	KIM Hui Yong
Min. of People's Security	RI Myong Su
Min. of Physical Culture & Sports	PAK Myong Chol
Min. of Post & Telecommunications	RYU Yong Sop
Min. of Procurement & Food Admin.	MUN Ung Jo
Min. of Public Health	CHOE Chang Sik
Min. of Railways	JON Kil Su
Min. of State Construction Control	PAE Tal Jun
Min. of State Inspection	KIM Ui Sun
Min. of Urban Management	HWANG Hak Won
Chmn., Capital Construction	KIM In Sik

Commission	
Chmn., Education Commission	KIM Yong Jin
Chmn., State Planning Commission	RO Tu Chol
Pres., State Academy of Sciences	JANG Chol
Dir., Central Statistics Bureau	KIM Chang Su
Pres., Central Bank	PAEK Ryong Chon
Permanent Representative to the UN, New York	SIN Son Ho

Political pressure groups and leaders:

> none

International organization participation:

> ARF, FAO, G-77, ICAO, ICC (NGOs), ICRM, IFAD, IFRCS, IHO, IMO, IOC, IPU, ISO, ITSO, ITU, NAM, UN, UNCTAD, UNESCO, UNIDO, UNWTO, UPU, WFTU (NGOs), WHO, WIPO, WMO

Diplomatic representation in the US:

> none; North Korea has a Permanent Mission to the UN in New York

Diplomatic representation from the US:

none; note - Swedish Embassy in Pyongyang represents the US as consular protecting power

Flag description:

three horizontal bands of blue (top), red (triple width), and blue; the red band is edged in white; on the hoist side of the red band is a white disk with a red five-pointed star; the broad red band symbolizes revolutionary traditions; the narrow white bands stands for purity, strength, and dignity; the blue bands signify sovereignty, peace, and friendship; the red star represents socialism

National symbol(s):

red star

National anthem:

name: "Aegukka" (Patriotic Song)

lyrics/music: PAK Se Yong/KIM Won Gyun

note: adopted 1947; both North Korea and South Korea's anthems share the same name and have a vaguely similar melody but have different lyrics; the North Korean anthem is also known as "Ach'imun pinnara" (Let Morning Shine)

Chapter 5: Economy

Economy - overview:

North Korea, one of the world's most centrally directed and least open economies, faces chronic economic problems. Industrial capital stock is nearly beyond repair as a result of years of underinvestment, shortages of spare parts, and poor maintenance. Large-scale military spending draws off resources needed for investment and civilian consumption. Industrial and power output have stagnated for years at a fraction of pre-1990 levels. Frequent weather-related crop failures aggravated chronic food shortages caused by on-going systemic problems, including a lack of arable land, collective farming practices, poor soil quality, insufficient fertilization, and persistent shortages of tractors and fuel. Large-scale international food aid deliveries have allowed the people of North Korea to escape widespread starvation since famine threatened in 1995, but the population continues to suffer from prolonged malnutrition and poor living conditions. Since 2002, the government has allowed private "farmers' markets" to begin selling a wider range of goods. It also permitted some private farming - on an experimental basis - in an effort to boost agricultural output. In December 2009, North Korea carried out a redenomination of its currency, capping the amount of North Korean won that could be exchanged for the new notes, and limiting the exchange to a one-week window. A concurrent crackdown on markets and foreign currency use yielded severe shortages and inflation, forcing Pyongyang to ease the restrictions by February 2010. In response to the sinking of the South Korean destroyer Cheonan and the shelling of Yeonpyeong Island, South Korea's government cut off most aid, trade, and bilateral cooperation activities, with the exception of operations at the Kaesong Industrial Complex. In 2012, KIM Jong Un's first year of leadership, the North displayed increased focus on the economy by renewing its commitment to special economic zones with China, negotiating a new payment structure to settle its $11 billion Soviet-era debt to Russia, and purportedly proposing new agricultural and industrial policies to boost domestic production. The North Korean government often highlights its goal of becoming a "strong and prosperous" nation and attracting foreign investment, a key factor for improving the overall standard of living. Nevertheless, firm political control remains the government's overriding concern, which likely will inhibit fundamental reforms of North Korea's current economic system.

GDP (purchasing power parity):

$40 billion (2011 est.)

country comparison to the world: 103

$40 billion (2010 est.)

$40 billion (2009 est.)

note: data are in 2011 US dollars;

North Korea does not publish reliable National Income Accounts data; the data shown here are derived from purchasing power parity (PPP) GDP estimates for North Korea that were made by Angus MADDISON in a study conducted for the OECD; his figure for 1999 was extrapolated to 2011 using estimated real growth rates for North Korea's GDP and an inflation factor based on the US GDP deflator; the results were rounded to the nearest $10 billion.

GDP (official exchange rate):

$28 billion (2009 est.)

GDP - real growth rate:

0.8% (2011 est.)

country comparison to the world: 170

-0.5% (2010 est.)

-0.9% (2009 est.)

GDP - per capita (PPP):

$1,800 (2011 est.)

country comparison to the world: 197

$1,800 (2010 est.)

$1,900 (2009 est.)

note: data are in 2012 US dollars

GDP - composition by sector:

agriculture: 23.1%

industry: 47.5%

services: 29.4% (2011 est.)

Labor force:

12.2 million

country comparison to the world: 44

note: estimates vary widely (2009 est.)

Labor force - by occupation:

agriculture: 35%

industry and services: 65% (2008 est.)

Budget:

revenues: $3.2 billion

expenditures: $3.3 billion (2007 est.)

Taxes and other revenues:

11.4% of GDP

country comparison to the world: 205

note: excludes earnings from state-operated enterprises (2007 est.)

Budget surplus (+) or deficit (-):

-0.4% of GDP (2007 est.)

country comparison to the world: 49

Inflation rate (consumer prices):

NA%

Agriculture - products:

rice, corn, potatoes, soybeans, pulses; cattle, pigs, pork, eggs

Industries:

military products; machine building, electric power, chemicals; mining (coal, iron ore, limestone, magnesite, graphite, copper, zinc, lead, and precious metals), metallurgy; textiles, food processing; tourism

Exports:

$4.707 billion (2011)

country comparison to the world: 117

$4.706 billion (2010 est.)

Exports - commodities:

minerals, metallurgical products, manufactures (including armaments), textiles, agricultural and fishery products

Exports - partners:

China 67.2%, South Korea 19.4%, India 3.6% (2011 est.)

Imports:

$4 billion (2011 est.)

country comparison to the world: 137

$2.934 billion (2010 est.)

Imports - commodities:

petroleum, coking coal, machinery and equipment, textiles, grain

Imports - partners:

China 61.6%, South Korea 20%, European Union 4% (2011 est.)

Debt - external:

$12.5 billion (2001 est.)

country comparison to the world: 87

Exchange rates:

North Korean won (KPW) per US dollar (market rate)

137 (2012 est.)

140 (2011 est.)

145 (2010 est.)

3,630 (December 2008)

140 (2007)

Fiscal year:

calendar year

Chapter 6: Energy

Electricity - production:

20.45 billion kWh (2009 est.)

country comparison to the world: 71

Electricity - consumption:

17.12 billion kWh (2009 est.)

country comparison to the world: 73

Electricity - exports:

0 kWh (2010 est.)

country comparison to the world: 213

Electricity - imports:

0 kWh (2010 est.)

country comparison to the world: 205

Electricity - installed generating capacity:

9.5 million kW (2009 est.)

country comparison to the world: 58

Electricity - from fossil fuels:

47.4% of total installed capacity (2009 est.)

country comparison to the world: 159

Electricity - from nuclear fuels:

0% of total installed capacity (2009 est.)

country comparison to the world: 119

Electricity - from hydroelectric plants:

52.6% of total installed capacity (2009 est.)

country comparison to the world: 39

Electricity - from other renewable sources:

0% of total installed capacity (2009 est.)

country comparison to the world: 143

Crude oil - production:

0 bbl/day (2011 est.)

country comparison to the world: 151

Crude oil - exports:

0 bbl/day (2009 est.)

country comparison to the world: 137

Crude oil - imports:

8,432 bbl/day (2009 est.)

country comparison to the world: 77

Crude oil - proved reserves:

0 bbl (1 January 2012 est.)

country comparison to the world: 150

Refined petroleum products - production:

9,133 bbl/day (2008 est.)

country comparison to the world: 106

Refined petroleum products - consumption:

15,070 bbl/day (2011 est.)

country comparison to the world: 145

Refined petroleum products - exports:

0 bbl/day (2008 est.)

country comparison to the world: 189

Refined petroleum products - imports:

7,967 bbl/day (2008 est.)

country comparison to the world: 137

Natural gas - production:

0 cu m (2010 est.)

country comparison to the world: 148

Natural gas - consumption:

0 cu m (2010 est.)

country comparison to the world: 160

Natural gas - exports:

0 cu m (2010 est.)

country comparison to the world: 97

Natural gas - imports:

0 cu m (2010 est.)

country comparison to the world: 87

Natural gas - proved reserves:

0 cu m (1 January 2012 est.)

country comparison to the world: 154

Carbon dioxide emissions from consumption of energy:

63.69 million Mt (2010 est.)

country comparison to the world: 53

Chapter 7: Communications

Telephones - main lines in use:

1.18 million (2011)

country comparison to the world: 72

Telephones - mobile cellular:

1 million (2011)

country comparison to the world: 155

Telephone system:

general assessment: adequate system; nationwide fiber-optic network; mobile-cellular service expanding beyond Pyongyang

domestic: fiber-optic links installed down to the county level; telephone directories unavailable; GSM mobile-cellular service initiated in 2002 but suspended in 2004; Orascom Telecom Holding, an Egyptian company, launched W-CDMA mobile service on December 15, 2008 for the Pyongyang area and has expanded service to several large cities

international: country code - 850; satellite earth stations - 2 (1 Intelsat - Indian Ocean, 1 Russian - Indian Ocean region); other international connections through Moscow and Beijing (2009)

Broadcast media:

no independent media; radios and TVs are pre-tuned to government stations; 4 government-owned TV stations; the Korean Workers' Party owns and operates the Korean Central Broadcasting Station, and the state-run Voice of Korea operates an external broadcast service; the government prohibits listening to and jams foreign broadcasts (2008)

Internet country code:

.kp

Internet hosts:

8 (2012)

<u>country comparison to the world</u>: 227

Chapter 8: Transportation

Airports:

>   81 (2012)

>   country comparison to the world: 71

Airports - with paved runways:

>   total: 39

>   over 3,047 m: 3

>   2,438 to 3,047 m: 22

>   1,524 to 2,437 m: 8

>   914 to 1,523 m: 2

>   under 914 m: 4 (2012)

Airports - with unpaved runways:

>   total: 42

>   2,438 to 3,047 m: 3

>   1,524 to 2,437 m: 17

>   914 to 1,523 m: 14

>   under 914 m: 8 (2012)

Heliports:

>   23 (2012)

Pipelines:

>   oil 154 km (2010)

Railways:

>   total: 5,242 km

>   country comparison to the world: 33

>   standard gauge: 5,242 km 1.435-m gauge (3,500 km electrified) (2009)

Roadways:

>   total: 25,554 km

>   country comparison to the world: 101

>   paved: 724 km

>   unpaved: 24,830 km (2006)

Waterways:

>   2,250 km (most navigable only by small craft) (2011)

>   country comparison to the world: 38

Merchant marine:

>   total: 158

>   country comparison to the world: 37

>   by type: bulk carrier 6, cargo 131, carrier 1, chemical tanker 1, container 4, passenger/cargo 1, petroleum tanker 12, refrigerated cargo 2

>   foreign-owned: 13 (Belgium 1, China 3, Nigeria 1, Singapore 1, South Korea 1, Syria 4, UAE 2)

>   registered in other countries: 6 (Mongolia 1, Sierra Leone 2, unknown 3) (2010)

Ports and terminals:

Ch'ongjin, Haeju, Hungnam (Hamhung), Namp'o, Senbong, Songnim, Sonbong (formerly Unggi), Wonsan

Chapter 9: Military

Military branches:

North Korean People's Army: Ground Forces, Navy, Air Force; civil security forces (2005)

Military service age and obligation:

17 years of age (2004)

Manpower available for military service:

males age 16-49: 6,515,279

females age 16-49: 6,418,693 (2010 est.)

Manpower fit for military service:

males age 16-49: 4,836,567

females age 16-49: 5,230,137 (2010 est.)

Manpower reaching militarily significant age annually:

male: 207,737

female: 204,553 (2010 est.)

Military expenditures:

NA

Chapter 10: Transnational Issues

Disputes - international:

risking arrest, imprisonment, and deportation, tens of thousands of North Koreans cross into China to escape famine, economic privation, and political oppression; North Korea and China dispute the sovereignty of certain islands in Yalu and Tumen rivers; Military Demarcation Line within the 4-km-wide Demilitarized Zone has separated North from South Korea since 1953; periodic incidents in the Yellow Sea with South Korea which claims the Northern Limiting Line as a maritime boundary; North Korea supports South Korea in rejecting Japan's claim to Liancourt Rocks (Tok-do/Take-shima)

Refugees and internally displaced persons:

IDPs: undetermined (flooding in mid-2007 and famine during mid-1990s) (2007)

Trafficking in persons:

current situation: North Korea is a source country for men, women, and children trafficked for the purposes of forced labor and commercial sexual exploitation; the most common form of trafficking involves North Korean women and girls who cross the border into China voluntarily; additionally, North Korean women and girls are lured out of North Korea to escape poor social and economic conditions by the promise of food, jobs, and freedom, only to be forced into prostitution, marriage, or exploitative labor arrangements once in China; within the country, North Koreans do not have a choice in the work the government assigns them and are not free to change jobs at will

tier rating: Tier 3 - North Korea does not fully comply with minimum standards for the elimination of trafficking and is not making significant efforts to do so; the government does not acknowledge the existence of human rights abuses in the country or recognize trafficking, either within the country or transnationally (2008)

Illicit drugs:

for years, from the 1970s into the 2000s, citizens of the Democratic People's Republic of (North) Korea (DPRK), many of them diplomatic employees of the government, were apprehended abroad while trafficking in narcotics, including two in Turkey in December 2004; police investigations in Taiwan and Japan in recent years have linked North Korea to large illicit shipments of heroin and methamphetamine, including an attempt by the North Korean merchant ship Pong Su to deliver 150 kg of heroin to Australia in April 2003

Other Key Facts™ Titles

Key Facts on Syria

Key Facts on China

Key Facts on Qatar

Key Facts on India

Key Facts on Germany

Key Facts on Argentina

Key Facts on Russia

Key Facts on North Korea

Key Facts on Brazil

Key Facts on Italy

Key Facts on the United Arab Emirates

Key Facts on the European Union

Key Facts on Pakistan

Key Facts on Saudi Arabia

Key Facts on Cyprus

Key Facts on Iran

Key Facts on Afghanistan

Key Facts on Iraq

THE INTERNATIONALIST®.
2013